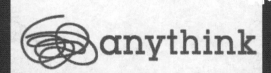

Makers as
INNOVATORS
JUNIOR

Gaming
with Bloxels

By Amy Quinn

CHERRY LAKE Publishing

Published in the United States of America by
Cherry Lake Publishing
Ann Arbor, Michigan
www.cherrylakepublishing.com

Series Editor: Kristin Fontichiaro
Reading Adviser: Marla Conn, MD, Ed., Literacy Specialist,
Read-Ability, Inc.
Photo Credits: All photos by Amy Quinn

Library of Congress Cataloging-in-Publication Data
Names: Quinn, Amy, 1976– author.
Title: Gaming with Bloxels / by Amy Quinn.
Description: Ann Arbor, Michigan : Cherry Lake Publishing, [2018] | Series: Makers
  as innovators junior | Audience: Grades K to 3. | Includes bibliographical references
  and index.
Identifiers: LCCN 2017032488 | ISBN 9781534107823 (lib. bdg.) | ISBN 9781534109803
  (pdf) | ISBN 9781534108813 (pbk.) | ISBN 9781534120792 (ebook)
Subjects: LCSH: Computer games—Programming—Juvenile literature. |
  Software patterns—Juvenile literature. | Bloxels (Trademark)—Juvenile literature.
Classification: LCC QA76.76.C672 Q56 2018 | DDC 005.1—dc23
  LC record available at https://lccn.loc.gov/2017032488

Cherry Lake Publishing would like to acknowledge the work of the Partnership for
21st Century Learning. Please visit *www.p21.org* for more information.

Printed in the United States of America
Corporate Graphics

A Note to Adults: Please review the instructions for the activities in this book before allowing children to do them. Be sure to help them with any activities you do not think they can safely complete on their own.

A Note to Kids: Be sure to ask an adult for help with these activities when you need it. Always put your safety first!

Table of Contents

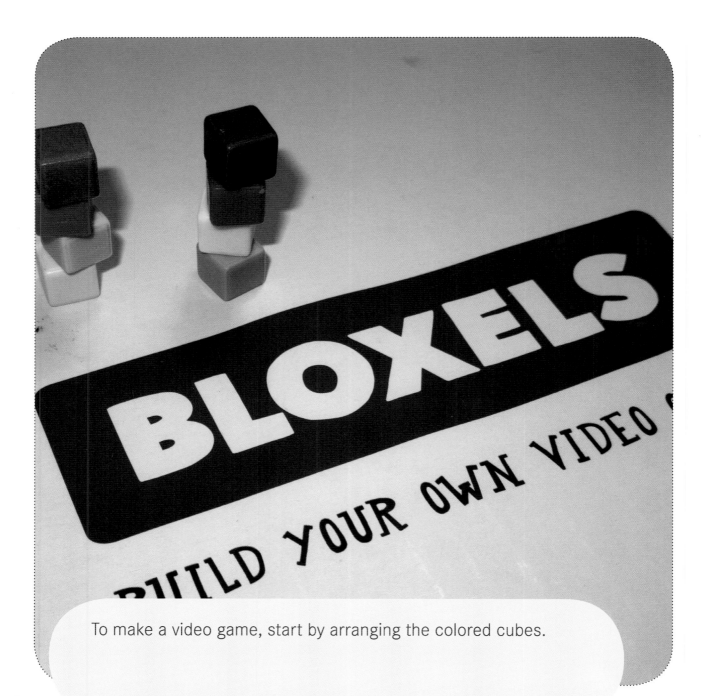

To make a video game, start by arranging the colored cubes.

Your Very Own Video Game

Do you love playing video games? Have you ever wanted to make your own game? Good news! You can easily design your own video game with Bloxels. Keep reading to find out how you can do this. You can create and play your video game. You can also share your game with your best friend. You can even share it with the whole world!

Arrange the plastic blocks on the game board. Then use your tablet to turn your design into a video game!

Getting Started

There are a few things you'll need to get started with Bloxels:

- Bloxels game board

- Set of Bloxels blocks

- A tablet or smartphone

- Bloxels Builder app

Internet Safety

The Bloxels Builder app is free. You can download it from your device's app store. But first, get permission and help from an adult. Create a username and password. Make sure to write them down!

You can place and move the blocks until you have a design you like.

Plan Your Game

Begin by planning your video game. Think of your game as a story. What are some fun characters you could include? They could be **imaginary**. They could also be based on real things. Where should your story take place? What is the problem? Is there an enemy? Let your imagination take over!

This boy is creating a game character called pizza man!

Building Layouts

Start by creating a **layout**. Each layout will be a room for your game. You can make up to 169 rooms per game. Use colorful blocks to build a layout. You put them on the game board **grid**. Each block color means something different. Add different blocks to make it harder for players!

Types of Blocks

Green—**terrain** block

Red—**hazard** block

Yellow—coin block

Purple—enemy block

Orange—exploding block

Gray—story block

Blue—water block

Pink—power-up block

Capturing your board is easy to do!

Capture a Game Board

Open the Bloxels Builder app. Find the picture of a camera and click on it. Take a picture of your game board. This is called capture. Snap! It is that easy. Now your layout is in the app. Want to change something? You can edit it in the app.

Tips for Capturing Your Layout

You might need to tip the camera to one side to capture a layout. Make sure you can see the entire game board. Change the camera brightness if needed. With a few tries, you will get it just right!

It is so fun to create characters!

Build Characters

Now your game needs some characters. It's time to build again! Use the blocks to build your character on the game board. Don't forget to add features such as legs, hands, and eyes. When your character is finished, open the app and capture it. Use the **animate** tool to make your character blink, walk, or jump. Your character will look like it came to life!

Can you see how the purple blocks in the background match up with the dragons in the game?

Play a Test Game

Now we're ready for the really fun part. Let's test your game! Give it a try. The arrow button moves your character left or right. Use the A button to attack and the B button to jump. What do you need to improve or change? What works well? Is the game too easy or too hard? Fix any problems and test it until it is just right!

How will you decorate your board?

Customize and Decorate

It is so much fun to **customize** and decorate your game using the Bloxels app. After you capture a layout, you can add art to the blocks. For example, the green blocks can be brown and green grass. The yellow blocks can be turned into coins. Just imagine it and make it! You can also make different **settings**. Create a house, sky, city, or underwater adventure!

Do you see a character you like? Add it to your game!

Infinity Wall

The Infinity Wall is a cool place to share your games and characters with others. Click on any empty space to add something. Select what you would like to share. See what other gamers have created. There are some great things on there! Use coins earned by playing to "purchase" items. This is also the place where you can follow other Bloxels users.

Anything Is Possible!

Remember that you can always change or add to your original idea. What types of games and characters do you and your friends enjoy? You could include a treasure, a dragon, a zombie, or even an original character.

Glossary

animate (AN-uh-mayt) to make something move

customize (KUHS-tuh-mize) to change something to suit a person's needs or interests

grid (GRID) a number of lines that form patterns of squares that are the same size

hazard (HAZ-urd) something that can be dangerous or cause problems for someone

imaginary (ih-MAJ-uh-ner-ee) existing in a world that is not real

layout (LAY-out) a plan or design of something laid out

settings (SEH-tingz) different places where a story takes place

terrain (tuh-RAYN) land

Find Out More

Books

Fontichiaro, Kristin. *Designing Board Games.* Ann Arbor, MI:
Cherry Lake Publishing, 2017.

Matteson, Adrienne. *Coding with ScratchJr.* Ann Arbor, MI:
Cherry Lake Publishing, 2017.

Web Sites

ABCYa—Pixel Art
www.abcya.com/pixel_art.htm
Make your own pixel art!

Scratch
https://scratch.mit.edu/projects/598125
Design your own game with Scratch!

Index

About the Author

Amy Quinn is a first grade teacher in West Bloomfield, Michigan. She is also a coach and mentor for FIRST LEGO League (FLL) and a team manager for Destination Imagination. Amy has a daughter, Emily, and a son, Tommy, who both love to design and create new things!